**LIVING SINGLE WITH A PURPOSE**

A Memoir

LYZA D. LEE

BEING *Single* IS OK!

Copyright © 2022 by Lyza D. Lee

All rights reserved. No part of this publication may be reproduced, distributed, or transmitted in any form or by any means, including photocopying, recording, or other electronic or mechanical methods, without the prior written permission of the publisher, except in the case of brief quotations embodied in critical reviews and certain other noncommercial uses permitted by copyright law.

# DEDICATION

*This book is dedicated to my mother, Loretta Patterson. Mom, you pushed me to complete this book because you knew it was a part of my destiny that would impact those that are before me and behind me.*

*It is done and I thank you!*

*I am so grateful to God, my creator, sustainer, father, and friend who designed my journey of singleness with love and sovereignty. He never left me and I shall never forget.*

> "FOR I KNOW THE PLANS I HAVE FOR YOU," DECLARES THE LORD, "PLANS TO PROSPER YOU AND NOT TO HARM YOU, PLANS TO GIVE YOU HOPE AND A FUTURE.
>
> ---
>
> JEREMIAH 29:11"

# CONTENTS

| | | |
|---|---|---|
| **INTRODUCTION** | | 1 |
| **The Journey: Part One** | What Was I Thinking? | 5 |
| **The Journey: Part Two** | What About Me? | 9 |
| **The Journey: Part Three** | Where Is This Going? | 20 |
| **The Journey: Part Four** | Singleness Is Amazing | 27 |
| **The Journey: Part Five** | This Is It ! | 33 |
| **Personal Journal Entry** | The Finale | 39 |
| **CONCLUSION** | | 42 |
| **ABOUT THE AUTHOR** | | 45 |
| **OVERVIEW AND CREDITS** | | 47 |

# INTRODUCTION

Many people struggle today with being single. Some have never been married like me, some are divorced, widowed, or too young to consider relationships but are curious.

Singleness is often viewed as a problem- meaning something has got to be wrong. With who? You or the other person? Usually, the finger is pointed at a single person.

The 'singleness' taboo phenomenon has escalated to the point that many single individuals choose not to do anything alone. Even if it means taking their BFF or someone close to that position to tag along for the sake of not being alone. This can create a frustrating question of 'why am I alone?' Why do I have to eat, sleep, live and travel alone? What is wrong with me? The list goes on.

Why, because many singles are not comfortable just being single.

This book is not an argument for anti-marriage. For you can be in a relationship (engaged, married, or not) and still be single; maybe not legally, but in so many other crucial ways.

So, I've heard. So, I've seen. And so, I certainly do not desire it.

In this book, I'm going to show you a wonderful discovery that being single really is ok.

Been there. Done that. Still doing it!!! At 57 years of age and still single (meaning never having been married), I speak from my heart and personal life experiences; the ups and downs, and uncertainties of the future. My future. Riding what seemed to be an emotional rollercoaster as my life took so many twists and turns! All the while trusting that God didn't forget me but was leading me down a path, He set for me. We all have our own paths. It's not one size fits all. And finally accepting a truth that for sure it's okay to be single.

This is more than a book; it's a memoir. It's a walkthrough of a 57-year journey of singleness while holding the hand of God. It permits you to be who God made you to be despite the negativity about being single. It sheds light on the many sides of singleness while providing a different perspective on being single with a God-given purpose to fulfill. It will challenge you to discover your path of singleness and see it as an opportunity to empower others to live life to the fullest as single,

## INTRODUCTION

whole and healthy individuals. Adopting this mindset can reduce anxiety, help you make better choices, and increase your satisfaction in life while preparing for the next chapter single or not. God has a plan and a purpose for everyone. Living single is purpose in the making.

Join me on this wonderful journey as I share authentic journal entries and experiences through 57 years of singleness ushering readers into being ok with who they are, where they are right now, and prepared for the wonderful changes that will come in their life.

Let's go!!

> **NEVER ALLOW SOMEONE TO BE YOUR PRIORITY WHILE ALLOWING YOURSELF TO BE THEIR OPTION**
>
> — MARK TWAIN

# THE JOURNEY: PART ONE

## WHAT WAS I THINKING?

---

**Being Single is OK Personal Journal Entries:**

Singleness is singleness past, present, and future. It doesn't matter if you are in a relationship or not, what's most important is being connected to yourself. Singleness is a state of having deliberate precedence over mental, physical, emotional, and yes even spiritual consciousness of who you are versus who you are connected to. What makes a total, complete, or whole person? How do you answer that question for yourself! The definition can and will change as you change, evolving into your best self and not because of someone else, but because of you, the one who should matter and the one you should love first.

It's funny, as I prepared to write this book that's been in the making for many years, I scrolled down through my computer personal files and found these two journal entries from eight years ago regarding my thoughts on my own singleness. I laughed thinking OMG I wrote this! Oh, and there are more to come as you continue to read on.

**I share these two journal entries with you, my readers; because I discovered them first and they are just as significant today as they were eight years ago.**

### Entry #1  6-17-14

I had a thought today as I prepared to celebrate my 50th birthday. Wow, never thought I would still be single (unmarried). Laughing out Loud (but not really). Not depressed. Not angry. Curious though. I understand the words that are now alive to me "God has a plan for your life and Proverbs 16:9 says "a man's heart plans his way but it is the Lord that directs his steps". Yep, those words are truly alive. I'm living them now. So, I conclude today that being single is really ok. It's a temporary lifestyle for some people like me and a permanent one for others. Is it a choice? Yes. Some would argue; others would not. I say we have an open-door policy with God our creator to chat about who we are, where we are, and why we are. He's faithful to answer and sometimes explain. Sometimes you wait. He is sure and that's for sure.

> *Appreciate where you are in your journey even if it's not where you want to be. Every season serves a purpose*
>
> ~ UNKNOWN

## Entry #2  6-19-14

I don't want to be just another single, just another woman, or just another person looking for fulfillment from another person. My purpose is in my spirit. I've got to live it. I've got to teach it. People must understand that all the good stuff God promised is just that. A promise was fulfilled. Along the way, on our journey, we are here to fulfill a God-given purpose; married or single. My quest in life is not marriage. It is to fulfill my purpose. The reason I'm here. I've got to do it and I am confident that again, all good stuff including marriage is in place for me.

> **ALONG THE WAY, ON OUR JOURNEY, WE ARE HERE TO FULFILL A GOD-GIVEN PURPOSE; MARRIED OR SINGLE.....**
>
> ---
>
> UNKNOWN

# THE JOURNEY: PART TWO

## WHAT ABOUT ME?

> *"I thought the formula was you finish school, graduate college, and get a good job…"*

There is a legitimate question on the table. Don't I matter? I know many singles have asked this question to themselves, to others, and even to God. At least I did.

I remember at 18 years of age, graduating high school and preparing to enter college, I soon became a caregiver in my home for my loved one. Life began to change drastically for me early on. By 19-20 years of age, I had a full-time job, enrolled in college, and was still caregiving. The thought of a relationship was looking bleak. I looked down the road of my life and couldn't see much more than what I saw at the present time. By the time I entered my mid to late 20s, the struggle became very real. Life had started to reveal itself in a way I didn't see coming.

My friends all around me were entering into relationships, becoming engaged, and setting wedding dates. I laughed because I could have opened a consignment store to sell all of my bridesmaid attire and make pretty good money. After all, I was in so many weddings; just not my own. All the while I'm thinking that my life looked a lot different from my friends. Why was that? I loved God. I was faithful to Him and the church. Yet I said to myself something is wrong with this picture. I didn't have a boyfriend. I didn't have a ring and I didn't have a wedding date. No funny conversations on the phone, no dates, no breakups, no make-ups, no anything but school, work, God, and caregiving. Yes, a few interests came and they went but never reached above the surface.

## The Formula

I'm not sure where it came from but many believed there was this magic formula of life and how it was supposed to go. During this phase of my life, I thought the formula was you finish school, graduate college, and get a good job. Now you're ready for marriage. You did everything you were supposed to. Marriage was supposed to just happen. The person would show up and that was it; Life happily ever after. I'm here to say that my plan and the formula failed miserably. I found myself almost 30 and still single. I recall one of my very young nieces said to me while we were in the kitchen one evening "auntie you mean you are 30 and you don't have a boyfriend! You need to put on some daisy dukes and that will do it" She was so young and innocent not really knowing much of anything but she knew enough to ask me that question. It was gut-wrenching. I wasn't about to put on daisy dukes to get a husband is what I said to her trying to explain something that she wouldn't understand until later in life. I had a moment after that question. It was unbelievable. Why was I this age and alone? I confess asking God 'hey what is up with this?'. Part of her statement was correct when she said you are at the age when you should have someone and you don't. Imagine a little girl not even in middle school yet thinking she has the solution to singleness for her 30-year-old aunt. Today I laugh, but back then it wasn't so funny; single with no sign of anything changing, questions pouring out of my heart, private pain. Wandering thoughts of How did I miss it? What's wrong with me? It's a good thing my private thoughts were not made into a movie. I'm sure the response would have been "seriously? "You mean to tell me you thought that way?" No one would believe I was capable of thinking such things. But I did.

As singles, pressures are all around us just because we are single; because someone is uncomfortable with our lifestyle. Some might call it selfish to think of you. I call it selfish NOT to think of you. All of this was ok with me, except I didn't fit anywhere into the picture other than meeting the need; Just not my own.

> *"People would be a lot better off if they'd enjoy being single."*

## Love takes time

> *"No one wants to experience that. Not me. No thanks."*

So, I decided that I would totally focus on loving two people; God and myself. I have always enjoyed listening to love ballads. Not sure why, but down through the years my heart and mind gravitated to lyrics and wonderful melodies. They allowed me to fantasize about love, being in love, breaking up, finding someone new, going through ups and downs, and staying together until we are old and gray.

The thought of so many songs of yesteryear makes me chuckle. Most of the stories of the songs I never experienced in real life; only in my dreams. It's funny because only later in life did songs evolve into focusing on one's self. They were hits in my opinion but truthfully could not compete with the powerful love ballads that society deemed iconic.

I'm not sure if I believe in love at first sight because I've never experienced that. I don't think I trust anyone to my heart quickly. That's just me. What I discovered while embracing love songs is that I needed to learn to love myself. That's not something you hear a lot of. But the truth is, I had nothing to offer anyone if I couldn't offer it to myself first.

Self-love is not selfish thinking, It's healthy reasoning. For many years the focus has been 'how not to be single'.

'What do I need to do to get someone's attention?'

'What do they want from me?' 'What are they looking for?'

I remember hearing so many of the things a man doesn't want so you better learn to do this and that. I realized that loving myself and figuring out what I wanted was just as important as what someone else might want from me. One day I asked myself a question. 'What do you want?'

I couldn't answer the question because it had not been my focus. I was busy with a lot of things and often put others' needs before my own.

I learned to help people, love them, take care of them and all the while put myself on the back burner thinking it was the right thing to do; only not for me.

I have attended so many singles conferences where you had an opportunity to meet other singles, and participate in different sessions, forums, and meetings all geared towards singles only. Explore the pros and cons of singleness, how to live holy while you wait on God to send that special someone into your life, find a mate, do fun activities together, etc. because it was of interest to me and a part of the ministry I was involved in at my local church serving in leadership in the youth department and various other ministries and single. I don't criticize the experience at all. But I grew weary of it. As a matter of fact, I could teach them myself. It seemed more of the same every time and I decided I was done with singles events altogether. Some people went out of their way to match up singles at the events. I hated that! I ran from it! It was entirely too uncomfortable. It opened the door for possible rejection. No one wants to experience that. Not me. No thanks.

One day, I heard a message titled 'Woman Thou Art Loosed' by Bishop T.D. Jakes. It changed my life, my perspective about singleness, and my self-image as a young woman, God's woman. The message encouraged women not to wait for a better half to be better to themselves, but to celebrate themselves and to look closely at who they are and know they have much to offer the world. Oh, I could go on and on about this wonderful series that rocked my world. There would be no quest to find love except within me and from above. I believed it would be worth the investment in me to learn how to love myself. I'm sure if you asked people what loving yourself means you would hear so many different things. If you asked me at that time, I would have probably said a lot of the same things others said. I was a young Christian girl who accepted Christ at the age of nine. I will never forget that Sunday when my mom went to the altar and rededicated her life to Christ, I was right there beside her. Didn't understand what I was doing other than getting saved. I watched my mom raise her hands to God and praise him for another opportunity to return and live for him. I wanted that too.

So, God became my God and my life. I stayed in and around the church. I grew in the Lord through study and teachings along with experiences. I found that as I became an adult, my commitment to God was rock solid. But when it came to communication I struggled, not knowing what to say when He and I were alone. Not at church during a regular service or a shut-in (which means you spend time with other believers usually at a church for a scheduled amount of uninterrupted time to give total attention to prayer), singing praises, teachings, and meditation before God or scheduled revival services where one could be spiritually fed and renewed; or at home alone with God whom I served. I needed a more intimate relationship with Him.

I didn't know how to develop that kind of walk that He and I would share alone; just the two of us. I loved God. I began to purchase books, and talk to those who were willing to share with me the wonderful things about God that I had yet to learn. As life began to take twists and turns my new journey began as I was challenged to trust God and depend on him as a God, friend, father, oh! the list goes on. Through my experiences, I got the intimacy I wanted which increased my love for God. While on this road a new challenge came about which was learning how to love myself. So many things can cause a person to not see themselves the way they should. You continue to beat yourself down for not living up to your own expectations.

Love is a journey. It doesn't matter who you love, it's still a journey that is defined as traveling from one place to another. That doesn't just mean geographically either. Most people don't know what it's like to be on a journey with yourself. We are accustomed to traveling in twos or more; never alone. On the journey of loving, there is time you give to yourself because you matter. Being content with being with yourself is vitally important to your overall health. Life will preoccupy you so much that by the time you try to think of yourself, you are exhausted. Your tank becomes empty then a lot of other things start happening and you don't even realize that you are missing yourself!

> *"To fall in love with yourself is the first secret to happiness."*
> ~ ROBERT MORELY

I remember many weekends I spent with me. I reserved the best hotel room that I could afford and that suited me. I enjoyed the food that pleased me, I did whatever I wanted to do because it was for me. Oh, it feels so good to love yourself and pay attention to everything about you. Believe it or not, God wants you to do that. When he said to love thy neighbor as thyself that meant you first have to love yourself in order to treat someone the way you treat you. How many of us will admit that we don't treat ourselves as best we should?

We go out of the way to please spouses, children, family members, bosses, friends, and so on. We take time to pick out great gifts, be there when we don't feel like it, listen, encourage, pray, and lift up, it doesn't stop. What if we did all those things for ourselves? What if we focused our attention on what we need and being fulfilled so that we will be in the position to help others without draining our tanks dry? Only when a tank is full can you give what is needed.

Many of us define time differently. We use this particular word daily. Some see time as some sort of restriction; others see it as an opportunity. Whatever the definition or reason, the question is: What does time mean to you? How does time affect your life?

Time is not negativity; it is a blessing. It gives us all a chance to ( you fill in the blank). We live in a 'microwave' world. This has, in so many ways, proved to be mentally harmful more than helpful. Sure, we want devices that will go faster, cars that beat the speed of light, red lights, and stop signs that need to disappear because we are in such a hurry for everything that nothing is worth waiting for. The time questions are often asked. Why does it take so long? Why do I /we have to wait? I'll pay to expedite whatever so the wait isn't so long. There is a famous saying "Ain't nobody got time for that!" Unfortunately, that's how we have been conditioned to live.

If anything is worth having, it is worth waiting for and that's a fact! There is a great risk in refusing to wait. That's not permission to do nothing; it's permission to do something! Waiting implies doing something until something else happens. Where you spend your efforts will determine your costs! Love can be the equivalent of a bottle of fine wine. It must go through its processes to become the best it was intended to be. It takes time but it's worth it in the end.

How much time are you willing to invest in yourself? What will it take to make sure that you know how much you love and appreciate yourself? A lot of time is spent reassuring others of our love and loyalty to them, which is not a bad thing at all. Giving to others takes a special heart in a selfish world. The focus, however, should not be on others while excluding you. Love takes time. Loving others takes time. Loving you takes time as well.

It is vitally important to our total health to be and remain aware of our own needs, the quest to only make someone else happy and feel fulfilled should be a thing of the past. Change is possible every day. Deciding to invest however much time needed in you is a worthy cause.

Being able to ask yourself hard questions such as what makes you happy, what you do for yourself, taking yourself on a date, or having a "me" day deserves a truthful heartfelt answer.

Think about sharing you with the world as one whole single unit, a real person, an individual completely in love with yourself, knowing who you are and being able to give all that you have to others as well as you, all because you took the time to love.

# "
# CHOICES
# EQUAL
# CONSEQUENCES

---

### D.M. JONES

# "

# THE JOURNEY: PART THREE

## WHERE IS THIS GOING?

---

> *"Walking in your purpose, especially single, brings double-loop roller coaster experiences"*

> *"The greatest tragedy in life is not death, but a life without purpose."*
> ~ Dr. Myles Munroe

## Purpose

Have you ever felt irritated and frustrated with where you are in life even though you know that you are right where you are supposed to be?

Walking in your purpose isn't always sunshine and roses. I recall reading a book on the subject of one's purpose and the first sentence said this: 'It's not about you!' I paused and then I laughed as I thought 'you got that right!' Had it been about me, I would not be in my position today doing singles ministry.

Thinking about your life while being single along with the emotional rollercoasters associated with being single can be cumbersome.

I remember as a girl my family always went to an amusement park on national holidays because my father had the day off and was a kid at heart. He would always say 'I grew up with my kids.' He enjoyed the park as much as we did! There was a huge roller coaster called the 'double loop' for those who were brave enough to try it. I tried it and it proved to be true to its word.

I, along with other riders, screamed and hollered as we went up and down, around and around, the thrill was just as crazy as it was scary. And when the loop part came around like a corkscrew it was like leaving your insides on the roller coaster track bouncing around. We always vowed never to take that ride again. But of course, we hopped back on that ride over and over again. Same fear, same challenge, same thrill. Single life and purpose are just like that ride! Just like a rollercoaster ride, life can take you up and down and all around. You are where you want to be, even when you say you don't.

## The Fear

Fear plagues each of us along the way, just like an unwanted partner who won't stop talking. You wake up in the morning and without any initiation, on your part, the thoughts appear. You are alone and you always will be. If I had a better job, more money, a better bodily figure, fewer health issues, a different car or home, nothing will ever change, oh if I could turn back the hands of time my life would be better but I can't. Fear freezes purpose and productivity. Many will never admit the reason they haven't moved forward is because of fear. Fear is not our friend; it's our enemy.

So how do we overcome fears and break the shackles that hold us back from walking in the God-given purpose that's already been assigned to us and sits upon our heads like a crown of gold? First of all, admission is a good thing. It's a part of becoming free. Making the first step by denouncing denial is a good thing. Make up your mind that I don't have to lie to myself about myself. On the other hand, you don't have to grab a microphone either and scream to the world I'm scared ok! When you are honest with yourself and God, you have just taken the first step. The good news is that God knows who you are, where you are, how you got there, and where you are going, for it is He that is our creator and our friend.

## The Challenge

Will I do it again or is it over for real? You make a decision, this is it. Then someone comes along and encourages you to try again. You remember the fear of the ride and yet being challenged somehow makes you rethink your decision to give up. Some live in the valley of decision, meaning they never seem to make up their mind about what they want to do. It's called living on the fence. And then some are rock solid in their decision-making process. When they say no it's no. Oh, there is the flexibility. I can do it again for personal reasons or not but I'm not struggling to decide. Someone on one of my jobs years ago anonymously sent me a wall posting that said Blessed are the flexible for they shall not be bent out of shape. I thought wow God sent this to me because this is what I needed to help me with my struggle of being able to bend like a pine tree amid a storm and still stand tall when it's all over. 25 years later I still have it because I still need it. Every day we walk in our purpose, and challenges are there to meet us. How we meet the challenge is a different story. It's first a thing of the mind. Wherever the mind goes, the body follows is my belief. Overcoming our thinking about ourselves is part of winning the battle. There is a Chinese proverb that says the journey of a thousand miles begins with one step.

## The Thrill

A well-known blues singer was famous for a song titled the thrill is gone! The thrill is gone! Those individuals who could relate to the song sang it with an understanding! It was a declared word that the thrill was there at one point but it's not anymore. It's over! Whatever I felt, it is no more! It's over for me and the double loop roller coaster. Any rollercoaster for that matter. I too can sing that song as it relates to the rollercoaster. But before it was over, I have to admit that with the fear of riding and the challenge of riding it again, there also was some type of thrill involved. Although hard to explain, it's very true.

As we, singles, live out our God-given purpose, it's important to know that it really is about Him and not us. That doesn't mean that we are insignificant in any way. What it does mean is that our God is the creator and sustainer of life. It is he who formed us in the womb. It is he who knows the hair count on our head. Our very heartbeat belongs to him. The purpose upon us was given to us by God. Walking in your purpose, especially single, brings double-loop roller coaster experiences. Some are good, fulfilling, and thrilling. Other times usher in fears and challenges. It's all a part of the journey. How would we be able to help anyone else if we didn't know the joys and pains of being single, unattached, walking with God, and living out our purpose? For those who come behind us, we are able to lift them, share our battles, show our scars and laugh about the joys of the journey.

Today I felt so much all at once; unusually indecisive about a lot of things. I was reminded that while I'm in the midst of life, loss, and love to let peace abound because I'm where I should be right now. It's a part of my path. Change is inevitable but it is not the focus. Someone once said wherever you are, be there! Staying in tune with God and yourself, and embracing those who bring words of life will help keep you on the path of purpose. From beginning to end, it is yours. Whatever God says we can do, we can. As long as he sought the Lord, he made him prosper... 2 Chronicles 26:5. Stay connected in every way, your purpose depends on it. If you abide in me and word abides in you, then you shall ask what you will and it shall be given to you.... John 15:7.

> SINGLENESS IS AN OPPORTUNITY TO EXPLORE LOVE; SELF-LOVE, GODLY LOVE, AND LOVE OF LIFE

— UNKNOWN

# THE JOURNEY: PART FOUR
## SINGLENESS IS AMAZING

Wow, look at each tree standing tall, full and bloomed and alone. Sure, other trees surrounded each tree, and yet there's only one trunk per tree. They looked calm and relaxed. They weren't depressed because they were the only ones in a large area. Their purpose was being fulfilled, standing strong, and providing shelter and oxygen.

Singleness is a God-given opportunity to express one's self and offer the world the great gift of you!

Singleness really is ok! It's not a permanent state of life but it is an important state of being. Before you invest time learning how to be a couple, learn how to be single. Bring the joy of wholeness to the table, not unhappiness. Dwelling on the unhappiness of single Dom sends the message 'unless I'm with someone, my life as a single is unimportant!' God never intended that to be; He honors marriage. As a matter of fact, it was He who instituted and ordained marriage stating in Genesis 2:18 "it is not good for man to be alone……."

Adam spent time single before Eve came on the scene. Adam had time to think! Who am I? Why am I here? Where am I? What is this or that? Adam explored his life, his existence, and his surroundings; without Eve.

So, it should be with singles. There are too many questions to be answered that don't include a significant other. Questions about you! Just like Adam, the first human. The quest for companionship has outweighed such an important piece of marriage. Our society has focused everything on twos. Restaurants, theaters, combos (charge more), travel, etc. The list goes on. They offer a false formula for how NOT to be single. Society is inundated with a shallow idea of marriage and couples. Singleness, one person, can give you a bad reputation in society and is criticized at times. It's almost a taboo to not be in a relationship of any kind. God understands the need for love and companionship. He values healthy relationships and perfect timing above all else. It is not his will for people to come together broken with the expectation of being fixed by the other person. It is not the responsibility of other people to heal you of past trauma. God is our healer. He wants us established; settled and happy with whom he made us be. Living life to its fullest with balance. Coming together, enhancing one another- continuing to fulfill life's purpose now as one single unit.

Singleness is Amazing!

> *"I like being single – I'm always there when I need me."*
> ~ ART LEO

## Self-love: Love Yourself

Self-image plays a significant part in our quest for singleness or companionship. How you see yourself as an individual is how you will see yourself once you are in a relationship. Singleness is an opportunity to explore love; Self-love, Godly love, and Love of life. Being unhappy with who you are not as a single person will put pressure on other people to validate you because you have not approved of yourself nor have you accepted God's approval of you which always was and will be because he made you. Jeremiah 1:5.

Self-love continues to be a challenge for everyone. We are constantly faced with the need to change; Hair, house, car, size, job, clothes, education. The list goes on. We are never enough. No matter who we are, what we have become, or what we will be; self-acceptance is key. I am who I am and that's who God made me to be. I am forever evolving into the best version of myself. I'm ok with me, Single or not. If there is a struggle to love and accept who a person is, then move on.

The question should be 'do you love me at all; Do I need to be who you want me to be before I can be?' The message sent is you are not ok. Change to satisfy me and then you will be ok. That is the wrong message. Singleness should always be combined with self-love and acceptance. It's ok. Really! Should singleness be permanent for me, my life still is fulfilling and complete. I still have 'me' to offer to the world and make a difference while balancing that with the love for not just myself but all those who are a part of my world. That's love worth having and sharing.

## Just Fly

One Sunday morning as I walked toward the church sanctuary door, I noticed a hawk and a bird in the sky. What a beautiful day they picked to have what I called "Sky drama". The hawk flew in circles and the little bird behind it. Round and round they went. I laughed and said 'hey little birdie you are no match for your opponent' suggesting there is a rift between them. Finally, the little bird flew away and let go. The hawk surprisingly continued to fly around and around. What beauty against the clear blue sky embraced by the sun? I wondered as I watched, what keeps that hawk in the air? No engine, no wheels, no pilot, no strings; nothing that would hold an aircraft in the air. The hawk, with long spread wings, continued to soar despite the earlier distraction of little birdie. Even after, it didn't stop. So, it should be with us. God made you to soar! Everything you need has been given. All of the gifting, abilities, and wisdom are present for you to dwell in your element. I'm sure during different seasons all the hawks get together as do birds of many kinds. There are times though that they all fly alone. Single, and yet they continue to soar. It is possible to walk in your own purpose as a single person and be successful as you do your part in building up the Kingdom of God. Be it you and you alone – Just Fly!

> **LOVE YOURSELF FIRST, BECAUSE THAT'S WHO YOU'LL SPEND THE REST OF YOUR LIFE WITH**
>
> — UNKNOWN

# THE JOURNEY: PART FIVE

## THIS IS IT !

---

> *"If not, careful, you will find yourself on an emotional trip that you didn't pack for…"*

## Calm Down

"So I like what I see when I'm looking at me when I'm walking past the mirror" is a line from the lyrics of the song Just Fine, 2007 Growing Pains album.

The validation of one's self is, in my opinion, the message of the song. The challenge is to take a deep look at who you are, explore the many levels and emotions of your being, move forward, and don't become a victim of someone else's opinion of you.

It's easy to hear and receive negative thoughts, and messages from people about who you are not and who or what you should be, and what you should be doing with your life. If not, careful, you will find yourself on an emotional trip that you didn't pack for which could easily lead to questioning yourself and being pressured mentally to make hasty decisions. There is a saying that haste makes waste and desperate people do desperate things which really is making emotional decisions that prove to be costly.

Take a deep breath now!

Did you know the many health benefits, physical, mental, and emotional, of deep breathing? It lowers your blood pressure, relieves anxiety, relaxes the body, and opens the door to a clear path of clarity in your mind to thinking clearly, evaluating, assessing, and making better decisions.

You owe it to yourself to do this. After all, it's your time and your life is given to you for a purpose to fulfill. Life-changing decisions shouldn't be made in 15 minutes with a 30-year lasting effect. It's equivalent to the nurturing of a seed planted that requires consistent watering, an appropriate amount of light, and pruning that produces a breath-taking beautiful plant to be enjoyed and to give and receive admiration. This is you! The seed that God planted on this beautiful earth with a wonderful purpose and plan just for you knowing that one day, in time, you will become all that you were meant to be. Take a moment to water yourself. Give you what you need to take in and absorb, feed your soil to eliminate dryness that could cause a quick decline; drink and be refreshed, and place yourself in a bright atmosphere, the natural light that works hand in hand with water to provide the necessary nutrients for growth. Allow the natural light, designed just for you, to shine life-giving rays. Before you know it, your leaves have blossomed and they stand tall and firm in awe and wonder!

> *"She remembered who she was and the game changed."*
> ~ LALAH DELIA

Now you sit in full bloom offering oxygen, beauty, joy, peace, and calmness to those who gaze upon you. The key is you must continue to feed yourself. That means in order to give, you must receive to be all you were designed to be from seed to plant.

Calm down.

## Filling The Moments

One of my mentors recently lost his companion for many years. This couple was engaged in purpose and balance. If ever there were a union close to perfection, in my opinion, they were it. I watched him after saying his final goodbye. Now he faced days of singleness after what seemed to be a lifetime of companionship; 61 years of marriage. He worked as diligently as before filling his day with important tasks to keep going.

I've also witnessed the in-between memories surfacing and him breaking down in tears, remembering everything about their life, especially the final moments. His daily challenge was dealing with never forgetting what they shared while moving forward with life. He functioned every day with human uncertainty of his future while spiritually dependent on God to heal his heart and to somehow laugh again. Living single, fulfilling a purpose, and developing balance is similar to this situation. Many singles haven't always been single. The list is long of why a person suddenly finds themselves single. Of course, some have always been single and yet whichever way it is, everyone still must fill in the moments.

What are the "moments"? A time where you gaze into the sunset or listen to the rainfall, maybe the beautiful diamond snowflakes and brutal cold holds you captive in the house. Whatever the scene, you are faced with thoughts, self-analysis, and questions with no answers.

What do you do with the difficult fleeting moments that would seem to come all too often? The bad news first; TV won't work for long, music may soothe…. depending. Eating won't help; crying is a healthy release but tends to physically drain and tax emotions but not discouraging.

A couple of important points to consider: This is a good time for positive self-talk. We can talk ourselves in and out of anything! Many times, our voice is the voice of reason, reflecting on our past, present, and desired future that only we know best; also incorporating God's will which covers every area of our lives. Yes, there is safety in a multitude of counselors..

> ..PROVERBS 11:14:
>
> *However, praying/talking to God first and alone keeps our focus and enhances our ability to hear words of comfort and even instruction.*

> *"Don't wait for someone else to shape your life. Shape it yourself."*
>
> ~ UNKNOWN

Denial is not a healthy part of singleness. It doesn't work. Guaranteed! Embracing reality, your true feelings that go along with singleness, balance, and purpose can lead you to a way of life that keeps you going and helps others follow your steps as you fill in the moments.

> TRUST IN THE LORD WITH ALL THINE HEART AND LEAN NOT UNTO THY OWN UNDERSTANDING. IN ALL THY WAYS ACKNOWLEDGE HIM AND HE SHALL DIRECT THY PATH

---

PROVERBS 3:5-6

# PERSONAL JOURNAL ENTRY

## THE FINALE

### April 11, 2022 @ 10:31 pm

In two and half months I will be blessed with having completed another full year of life; a gift from my Lord, creator, and happily my Father and friend. 57 years to be exact! And yes, I am still single. By way of a familiar definition; unmarried, never being engaged, walking the grand isle, tasted wedding cake of my own, danced until I gave out at my wedding reception, and waved see you soon to all of my family and friends as I was dashed off into the sunset to the end of singleness and the beginning of the marriage. But wait, oh no, hold up, I dare not leave it like that lol. Absolutely not! I'm single, yes, as I fore stated by way of the common definition but also by way of my definition, the one that describes not my marital connection but my excitement yet again of another year of life, actually living my best life, journeying still, embracing 58 years young and an absolute fanatic about what is yet to come in my life for me. You know those dreams we dream about; some we talk about and hopefully push ourselves to do something about. I'm happy because I am me. I really like me as I chuckle thinking of the very distant past about times when I didn't. Well hallelujah I do now. I have so many things on my mind. Stuff I want to do and have purposed in my heart and mind that I will do. Finishing this memoir is a priority. My desire to share my purposeful journey of how loving myself puts me in the optimal position to achieve all I want to and God wants me to because I can. It's my life and my dream along with all of the hopes and even the fears. What is life without all of those ingredients and events that shape us into that wonderful dessert to be shared with and enjoyed by so many who will taste, digest, and have all those nutrients that will help them become their best self too! So, when the time comes for you to be shared with whomever God should allow to cross your path, they will dine sufficiently on the best you that you were created to be.

Bon Appetit.

> TWO MOST IMPORTANT DAYS ARE THE DAY YOU ARE BORN AND THE DAY YOU FIND OUT WHY.

— MARK TWAIN

# CONCLUSION
## THE POWER OF CHOICE

The fact that you were born is proof that you have something special already within you before you entered the world; crossed over into time.

It's not enough to be here. To merely exist, to float through life and give everyone and everything the best of you except to you! A giving heart is a beautiful thing. To those who are givers and those who have yet to discover. Giving in some way is a part of everyone's purpose in life, I believe. No greater feeling of achievement is there to know you made a difference! The value has no dollar sign. Regardless of the challenges that come with fulfilling your purpose; knowing it's a part of your path gives you the strength to stay true to it.

Valuing one's self is significantly important to fulfilling your purpose. How can you love and help anyone if you don't start with yourself? You cannot truly give what you don't have to give. "-love thy neighbor as thyself…"-Matthew 22:39. None of this has to do with the person or individuals to come on the scene in your future. You are the first one here! Single.

What then do you do? You do you! Love you! Love you! Be thankful for your life! Give all to you that you would give to others. Be a recipient of God's love that teaches you about love and shows you about love, especially self-love. Take as much time as you need to reach within, find out who you are, and what you like, discover and identify your strengths and weaknesses, and be accepting of yourself; take action on your desires for yourself with wisdom. There is an African proverb that says man, know thyself. It speaks to us all, male and female. It's best to know you first before investing in someone else. Knowing you gives you the advantage, and stability and dispels those who would seek to take advantage of your God-given inward beauty, abuse it and tear it down like an abandoned building marked condemned.

Use all of you, the whole you, experiences of ups and downs, your process of learning you, accepting you as building blocks preparing to share you with you and others continue on the journey that started with you and will last through you one day leaving a wonderful legacy that I came, I became and I will forever be single, whole and complete. And it's okay!

> "EVERY SINGLE MOMENT SHAPES OUR FUTURE. BE INTENTIONAL. LIVE ON PURPOSE"
>
> —— UNKNOWN

# ABOUT THE AUTHOR

**Ms. Lyza D. Lee** is a new author inspired to encourage and motivate individuals to effective daily living through practical teaching. Ms. Lee has, as a single of 57 years, addressed spirit relational issues through many teaching and training opportunities. The central theme of her message is we must put God first and love him before we can love anyone else including ourselves. She is the founder and president of HML, Inc. She is also the author of From the Heart Poetry collection soon to be published. Ms. Lee has also functionped in many community-based leadership positions and locally in her church. She is a graduate of The University of Akron and has also completed numerous continuing education courses and participated in multiple leadership training classes. Ms. Lee is currently still single and serving God.

> **YOU ARE NOT IMPORTANT BECAUSE OF HOW LONG YOU LIVE, YOU ARE IMPORTANT BECAUSE OF HOW EFFECTIVE YOU LIVE.**
>
> — UNKNOWN

# OVERVIEW AND CREDITS
# SINGLENESS: LOVING YOU FIRST

Men and women of every culture are faced with the pressures of daily living; even survival. Unfortunately, with that also comes the pressure of singleness. Why are you single? Do you want to be single? What does it mean to be single? What is God's take on singleness? There are so many unanswered questions about being alone or not. Ms. Lee examines singles from two perspectives and offers self-help tips from her life's experiences and God's word to any and everyone who needs assurance that being single is OK.

## BOOK CREDITS

*As a woman this book is truly a balm over sore wounds. Society is constantly pressuring us to do and be people that we are not. Self care is definitely not talked about enough especially among women in regards to societal gender roles and norms. It is time to start loving ourselves and being kind to ourselves first and foremost before looking for relationships with others whether it be romantic or Platonic. This memoir really struck a chord with me and the author is so intentional and thoughtful throughout the book. This body of work encourages you to stop and take a look in the mirror. This book is the perfect mix of humor, empathy, and self reflection! You definitely want this book in your library, it is a gift both to yourself and to people around you! Don't pass this book up!*

~ DR SADE CROWLEY AU.D, B.S, AAA

*Ms. Lee does not offer theory or speculation. She speaks from decades of experiences in life and inspirations from God's holy word. Her book debunks the utopian fantasies of people who presume to know what single people need, using the life experiences she has experienced herself. Lyza gives voice to singleness. She tells her story. Give it a read ----it's enthralling.*``

~ GARY L WYATT SR,
Author: From Dealing to Healing
www.northhillcommunityhouse.org

*The writer of this book is transparent and powerful . Her words are reassuring, causing the reader to become self assured . It is a resource that I can use on my journey to becoming a better me.*

~ EVANGELIST MARVIN J. MCDANIEL

Being Single Is Okay! A great curriculum guide to explore the *concepts of "self Love," "God Love" and "Love of Life."* Another tool to help connect Singles thru bible study, book discussion topics and community outreach groups.--

**PASTORS PAUL AND DIANE JACKSON,**
Cascade Faith Ministries, Inc. Akron, OH

*This book is not only an excellent read but powerful in its delivery reaching not only intellectual awareness but also captures one's soul. Minds will be challenged and values will be changed as a result of this book. How proud I am to see you bring value to our ever so confused world. This book is definitely a tool for every person single and married. The example of courage Lyza shares with us is nothing short of amazing. This is a start of things to come and I'm definitely going along for the ride. Congratulations!*

**JAMIE L. PATTERSON, JR**
Entrepreneur

Made in the USA
Middletown, DE
28 October 2024